LESSONS *from* LEGENDS

Powerful Life Principles
from Thirteen Compelling Bible Characters

MARK RASMUSSEN

First published in 2011 by Striving Together Publications, a ministry of Lancaster Baptist Church, Lancaster, CA 93535. Striving Together Publications is committed to providing tried, trusted, and proven books that will further equip local churches to carry out the Great Commission. Your comments and suggestions are valued.

Striving Together Publications
4020 E. Lancaster Blvd.
Lancaster, CA 93535
800.201.7748

Cover design by Andrew Jones
Layout by Craig Parker
Edited by David Coon
Special thanks to our proofreaders.

ISBN 978-1-59894-165-4

Printed in the United States of America

TABLE OF CONTENTS

JOSHUA
Training for Leadership

Text

JOSHUA 1:1–8

1   Now after the death of Moses the servant of the LORD it came to pass, that the LORD spake unto Joshua the son of Nun, Moses' minister, saying,

2   Moses my servant is dead; now therefore arise, go over this Jordan, thou, and all this people, unto the land which I do give to them, even to the children of Israel.

3   Every place that the sole of your foot shall tread upon, that have I given unto you, as I said unto Moses.

4   From the wilderness and this Lebanon even unto the great river, the river Euphrates, all the land of the Hittites, and unto the great sea toward the going down of the sun, shall be your coast.

5   There shall not any man be able to stand before thee all the days of thy life: as I was with Moses, so I will be with thee: I will not fail thee, nor forsake thee.

6   Be strong and of a good courage: for unto this people shalt thou divide for an inheritance the land, which I sware unto their fathers to give them.

7   Only be thou strong and very courageous, that thou mayest observe to do according to all the law, which Moses my servant commanded thee: turn not from it to the right hand or to the left, that thou mayest prosper whithersoever thou goest.

8   This book of the law shall not depart out of thy mouth; but thou shalt meditate therein day and night, that thou mayest observe to do according to all that is written therein: for then thou shalt make thy way prosperous, and then thou shalt have good success.

Overview

Much of our learning comes through the power of examples. Therefore, the wise Christian will deliberately find godly examples and follow them. In Joshua we see a man who spent years in preparation under a great leader, and so became fit to become the leader himself in God's own time.

Lesson Theme

We think of Joshua as a great warrior, whose power and success were due to the blessing of God on his life. At the same time, it is important for us to see that Joshua was a trained and prepared man as well. God used Joshua's time of training under Moses to prepare him for the leadership of the nation. If we will take the time and effort to become prepared, God will be able to use us more effectively as well.

Introduction

_____

_____

_____

I.   Serving the _____

JOSHUA 1:1

1   Now after the death of Moses the servant of the LORD it came to pass, that the LORD spake unto Joshua the son of Nun, Moses' minister, saying…

A.   FAITHFUL TO _____

EXODUS 24:13–14

13   And Moses rose up, and his minister Joshua: and Moses went up into the mount of God.

14   And he said unto the elders, Tarry ye here for us, until we come again unto you: and, behold, Aaron and Hur are with you: if any man have any matters to do, let him come unto them.

EXODUS 32:15–17

15   And Moses turned, and went down from the mount, and the two tables of the testimony were in his hand: the tables were written on both their sides; on the one side and on the other were they written.

16   And the tables were the work of God, and the writing was the writing of God, graven upon the tables.

17   And when Joshua heard the noise of the people as they shouted, he said unto Moses, There is a noise of war in the camp.

B. **FAITHFUL TO** _____

EXODUS 17:8–13

8   Then came Amalek, and fought with Israel in Rephidim.

9   **And Moses said unto Joshua, Choose us out men, and go out, fight with Amalek:** to morrow I will stand on the top of the hill with the rod of God in mine hand.

10   So Joshua did as Moses had said to him, and fought with Amalek: and Moses, Aaron, and Hur went up to the top of the hill.

11   And it came to pass, when Moses held up his hand, that Israel prevailed: and when he let down his hand, Amalek prevailed.

12   But Moses' hands were heavy; and they took a stone, and put it under him, and he sat thereon; and Aaron and Hur stayed up his hands, the one on the one side, and the other on the other side; and his hands were steady until the going down of the sun.

13   And Joshua discomfited Amalek and his people with the edge of the sword.

II. Seeking the _____

JOSHUA 1:2–5

2   Moses my servant is dead; now therefore arise, go over this Jordan, thou, and all this people, unto the land which I do give to them, even to the children of Israel.

3   Every place that the sole of your foot shall tread upon, that have I given unto you, as I said unto Moses.

4   From the wilderness and this Lebanon even unto the great river, the river Euphrates, all the land of the Hittites, and unto the great sea toward the going down of the sun, shall be your coast.

5   *There shall not any man be able to stand before thee all the days of thy life:* **as I was with Moses, so I will be with thee: I will not fail thee, nor forsake thee.**

A. _____

NUMBERS 14:6–9

6   *And Joshua the son of Nun, and Caleb the son of Jephunneh, which were of them that searched the land, rent their clothes:*

7   *And they spake unto all the company of the children of Israel, saying, The land, which we passed through to search it, is an exceeding good land.*

8   **If the LORD delight in us, then he will bring us into this land, and give it us;** *a land which floweth with milk and honey.*

9   **Only rebel not ye against the LORD,** *neither fear ye the people of the land; for they are bread for us: their defence is departed from them, and the LORD is with us: fear them not.*

B. _____

JOSHUA 5:13–6:5

13   *And it came to pass, when Joshua was by Jericho, that he lifted up his eyes and looked, and, behold, there stood a man over against him with his sword drawn in his hand: and Joshua went unto him, and said unto him, Art thou for us, or for our adversaries?*

14   *And he said, Nay; but as captain of the host of the LORD am I now come. And Joshua fell on his face to the earth, and did worship, and said unto him, What saith my lord unto his servant?*

15 And the captain of the Lord's host said unto Joshua, Loose thy shoe from off thy foot; for the place whereon thou standest is holy. And Joshua did so.

6:1 Now Jericho was straitly shut up because of the children of Israel: none went out, and none came in.

2 And the Lord said unto Joshua, See, I have given into thine hand Jericho, and the king thereof, and the mighty men of valour.

3 And ye shall compass the city, all ye men of war, and go round about the city once. Thus shalt thou do six days.

4 And seven priests shall bear before the ark seven trumpets of rams' horns: and the seventh day ye shall compass the city seven times, and the priests shall blow with the trumpets.

5 And it shall come to pass, that when they make a long blast with the ram's horn, and when ye hear the sound of the trumpet, all the people shall shout with a great shout; and the wall of the city shall fall down flat, and the people shall ascend up every man straight before him.

Joshua 8:1–7

1 And the Lord said unto Joshua, Fear not, neither be thou dismayed: take all the people of war with thee, and arise, go up to Ai: see, I have given into thy hand the king of Ai, and his people, and his city, and his land:

2 And thou shalt do to Ai and her king as thou didst unto Jericho and her king: only the spoil thereof, and the cattle thereof, shall ye take for a prey unto yourselves: lay thee an ambush for the city behind it.

3   *So Joshua arose, and all the people of war, to go up against Ai: and Joshua chose out thirty thousand mighty men of valour, and sent them away by night.*

4   *And he commanded them, saying, Behold, ye shall lie in wait against the city, even behind the city: go not very far from the city, but be ye all ready:*

5   *And I, and all the people that are with me, will approach unto the city: and it shall come to pass, when they come out against us, as at the first, that we will flee before them,*

6   *(For they will come out after us) till we have drawn them from the city; for they will say, They flee before us, as at the first: therefore we will flee before them.*

7   *Then ye shall rise up from the ambush, and seize upon the city: for the Lord your God will deliver it into your hand.*

III. Conquering a _____

Joshua 1:6–8

6   **Be strong and of a good courage: for unto this people shalt thou divide for an inheritance the land, which I sware unto their fathers to give them.**

7   *Only be thou strong and very courageous, that thou mayest observe to do according to all the law, which Moses my servant commanded thee: turn not from it to the right hand or to the left, that thou mayest prosper whithersoever thou goest.*

8   *This book of the law shall not depart out of thy mouth; but thou shalt meditate therein day and night, that thou mayest observe to do according to all that is written therein: for then thou shalt make thy way prosperous, and then thou shalt have good success.*

A. The land was _____.

Numbers 13:31–33

31 But the men that went up with him said, We be not able to go up against the people; for they are stronger than we.

32 And they brought up an evil report of the land which they had searched unto the children of Israel, saying, The land, through which we have gone to search it, is a land that eateth up the inhabitants thereof; and all the people that we saw in it are men of a great stature.

*33 **And there we saw the giants, the sons of Anak, which come of the giants: and we were in our own sight as grasshoppers, and so we were in their sight.***

B. The Lord was _____.

Joshua 6:7

7 And he said unto the people, Pass on, and compass the city, and let him that is armed pass on before the ark of the Lord.

Joshua 6:20

*20 So the people shouted when the priests blew with the trumpets: and it came to pass, when the people heard the sound of the trumpet, and the people shouted with a great shout, that the wall fell down flat, so that the people went up into the city, every man straight before him, **and they took the city.***

Conclusion

Study Questions

1. Who was the man Joshua followed? List some examples of Joshua's "follow-ship."

2. Finish this thought: Before one can expect to become a leader, he or she must first spend time as a _____.

3. Describe Joshua's first expedition into the Promised Land.

4. Where did Joshua get his encouragement and his battle plan for the conquest of Jericho?

5. Where and why did Joshua meet his greatest defeat?

6. How should you react to the inevitable problems and even dangers that come as you seek to serve God?

7. What was the basis of Joshua's firm belief that the victory would be won?

8. What are some practical ways in which we can follow the steps of Joshua?

Memory Verse

This book of the law shall not depart out of thy mouth; but thou shalt meditate therein day and night, that thou mayest observe to do according to all that is written therein: for then thou shalt make thy way prosperous, and then thou shalt have good success.
—JOSHUA 1:8

CALEB
Mountain Claiming

Text

JOSHUA 14:6–12

6 Then the children of Judah came unto Joshua in Gilgal: and Caleb the son of Jephunneh the Kenezite said unto him, Thou knowest the thing that the LORD said unto Moses the man of God concerning me and thee in Kadeshbarnea.

7 Forty years old was I when Moses the servant of the LORD sent me from Kadeshbarnea to espy out the land; and I brought him word again as it was in mine heart.

8 Nevertheless my brethren that went up with me made the heart of the people melt: but I wholly followed the LORD my God.

9 And Moses sware on that day, saying, Surely the land whereon thy feet have trodden shall be thine inheritance, and thy children's for ever, because thou hast wholly followed the LORD my God.

10 And now, behold, the LORD hath kept me alive, as he said, these forty and five years, even since the LORD spake this word unto Moses, while the children of Israel wandered in the wilderness: and now, lo, I am this day fourscore and five years old.

11 As yet I am as strong this day as I was in the day that Moses sent me: as my strength was then, even so is my strength now, for war, both to go out, and to come in.

12 Now therefore give me this mountain, whereof the LORD spake in that day; for thou heardest in that day how the Anakims were there, and that the cities were great and fenced: if so be the LORD will be with me, then I shall be able to drive them out, as the LORD said.

Overview

In Caleb we see an example of a faithful man who first believed the promise of God, then trusted Him through forty-five years of good times and bad times, and finally claimed that promise for the glory of God.

Lesson Theme

Caleb wanted his mountain, but he was willing to wait for decades to claim the promise of God and to achieve his goal in God's time and God's way. We, too, need to believe God enough to trust that His way is always best and that He will do the right thing at exactly the right time.

Introduction

_____

_____

_____

I. Relied on _____

PSALM 119:11, 105

11 Thy word have I hid in mine heart, that I might not sin against thee.

105 Thy word is a lamp unto my feet, and a light unto my path.

EZRA 7:10

10 For Ezra had prepared his heart to seek the law of the LORD, and to do it, and to teach in Israel statutes and judgments.

A. As a _____

JOSHUA 14:6–8

6 Then the children of Judah came unto Joshua in Gilgal: and Caleb the son of Jephunneh the Kenezite said unto him, Thou knowest the thing that the LORD said unto Moses the man of God concerning me and thee in Kadesh-barnea.

7 Forty years old was I when Moses the servant of the LORD sent me from Kadesh-barnea to espy out the land; and I brought him word again as it was in mine heart.

*8 Nevertheless my brethren that went up with me made the heart of the people melt: **but I wholly followed the LORD my God.***

B. As a _____

II. Remained _____

A. _____

NUMBERS 14:24

*24 But **my servant Caleb**, because he had another spirit with him, and hath followed me fully, him will I bring into the land whereinto he went; and his seed shall possess it.*

B. _____

NUMBERS 14:24

*24 But my servant Caleb, because he had another spirit with him, and **hath followed me fully**, him will I bring into the land whereinto he went; and his seed shall possess it.*

III. Remembered the _____

A. THE PROMISE OF THE _____

JOSHUA 14:12

*12 Now therefore give me this mountain, **whereof the LORD spake in that day**; for thou heardest in that day how the Anakims were there, and that the cities were great and fenced: if so be the LORD will be with me, then I shall be able to drive them out, as the LORD said.*

ACTS 27:25

25 Wherefore, sirs, be of good cheer: for I believe God, that it shall be even as it was told me.

B. THE PROMISE OF THE _____

JOSHUA 14:12

*12 Now therefore give me this mountain, **whereof the LORD spake in that day**; for thou heardest in that day how the Anakims were there, and that the cities were great and fenced: if so be the LORD will be with me, **then I shall be able to drive them out, as the LORD said**.*

C. THE PROMISE OF THE _____

JOSHUA 14:9–12

9 And Moses sware on that day, saying, Surely the land whereon thy feet have trodden shall be thine inheritance, and thy children's for ever, because thou hast wholly followed the LORD my God.

10 And now, behold, the Lord hath kept me alive, as he said, these forty and five years, even since the LORD spake this word unto Moses, while the children of Israel wandered in the wilderness: and now, lo, I am this day fourscore and five years old.

11 As yet I am as strong this day as I was in the day that Moses sent me: as my strength was then, even so is my strength now, for war, both to go out, and to come in.

12 Now therefore give me this mountain, whereof the LORD spake in that day; for thou heardest in that day how the Anakims were there, and that the cities were great and fenced: if so be the LORD will be with me, then I shall be able to drive them out, as the LORD said.

Conclusion

Study Questions

1. How old was Caleb when he said, "Give me this mountain"? How long had he waited to claim God's promise?

2. What is to be the GPS of the Christian's life?

3. How did the Lord Jesus Christ counter the temptations of Satan?

4. What Bible chapter is especially filled with examples of people who had faith and were faithful to God in challenging circumstances?

5. Realizing that the Bible states that Caleb "wholly followed the LORD," how would you rate yourself on following the Lord (on a scale of one to ten)?

6. What promises of God are especially meaningful to you?

7. Where do you especially need victory in your life right now?

8. What promises of God would apply to this area where you need victory?

Memory Verse

Now therefore give me this mountain, whereof the LORD spake in that day; for thou heardest in that day how the Anakims were there, and that the cities were great and fenced: if so be the LORD will be with me, then I shall be able to drive them out, as the LORD said.—JOSHUA 14:12

BARNABAS
The Encourager

Text

ACTS 11:22–26

22 Then tidings of these things came unto the ears of the church which was in Jerusalem: and they sent forth Barnabas, that he should go as far as Antioch.

23 Who, when he came, and had seen the grace of God, was glad, and exhorted them all, that with purpose of heart they would cleave unto the Lord.

24 For he was a good man, and full of the Holy Ghost and of faith: and much people was added unto the Lord.

25 Then departed Barnabas to Tarsus, for to seek Saul:

26 And when he had found him, he brought him unto Antioch. And it came to pass, that a whole year they assembled themselves with the church, and taught much people. And the disciples were called Christians first in Antioch.

Overview

Barnabas was a man who worked mainly behind the scenes. He was a generous man in the cause of the Lord, not only in the matter of his finances but also in his personal influence. He was one who took the time and effort to encourage people, and in fact the very name Barnabas means "the son of consolation." In particular, God used him to rescue and restore his nephew John Mark, who had been dismissed from Paul's missionary team.

Lesson Theme

All of us need encouragement from time to time, and we all remember times when a little encouragement made a great difference to us. Perhaps we can also recall times when we were used by God to encourage someone else, and what a blessing that was to us as well. Through the scriptural narrative of several incidents in the life of Barnabas, we will see how we can be encouragers whom God can use to be great positive influences on the lives of others.

Introduction

_____

_____

_____

I. _____ to God

A. _____

ACTS 4:36–37

36 And Joses, who by the apostles was surnamed Barnabas, (which is, being interpreted, The son of consolation,) a Levite, and of the country of Cyprus,
37 Having land, sold it, and brought the money, and laid it at the apostles' feet.

LUKE 6:38

38 Give, and it shall be given unto you; good measure, pressed down, and shaken together, and running over, shall men give into your bosom. For with the same measure that ye mete withal it shall be measured to you again.

MALACHI 3:10–11

10 Bring ye all the tithes into the storehouse, that there may be meat in mine house, and prove me now herewith, saith the LORD of hosts, if I will not open you the windows of heaven, and pour you out a blessing, that there shall not be room enough to receive it.
11 And I will rebuke the devourer for your sakes, and he shall not destroy the fruits of your ground; neither shall your vine cast her fruit before the time in the field, saith the LORD of hosts.

B. _____

ACTS 9:27

27   But Barnabas took him, and brought him to the apostles, and declared unto them how he had seen the Lord in the way, and that he had spoken to him, and how he had preached boldly at Damascus in the name of Jesus.

2 TIMOTHY 2:2

2   And the things that thou hast heard of me among many witnesses, the same commit thou to faithful men, who shall be able to teach others also.

II.   _____ the Saints

MATTHEW 20:26–28

26 But it shall not be so among you: but whosoever will be great among you, let him be your minister;
27 And whosoever will be chief among you, let him be your servant:
28 Even as the Son of man came not to be ministered unto, but to minister, and to give his life a ransom for many.

A. EXHORTED THE _____

ACTS 11:23

*23 Who, when he came, and had seen the grace of God, was glad, **and exhorted them all**, that with purpose of heart they would cleave unto the Lord.*

B. ENCOURAGED HIS _____

ACTS 11:25–26

25 Then departed Barnabas to Tarsus, for to seek Saul:

26 And when he had found him, he brought him unto Antioch. And it came to pass, that a whole year they assembled themselves with the church, and taught much people. And the disciples were called Christians first in Antioch.

LUKE 19:10
10 For the Son of man is come to seek and to save that which was lost.

1. **He loved the unlovely.**

2. **He loved the Gentiles.**
   ACTS 15:12
   12 Then all the multitude kept silence, and gave audience to Barnabas and Paul, declaring what miracles and wonders God had wrought among the Gentiles by them.

III. _____ the Rebuked (John Mark)

A. _____ JOHN MARK

ACTS 15:36–39
36 And some days after Paul said unto Barnabas, Let us go again and visit our brethren in every city where we have preached the word of the Lord, and see how they do.
37 And Barnabas determined to take with them John, whose surname was Mark.
38 But Paul thought not good to take him with them, who departed from them from Pamphylia, and went not with them to the work.

39 And the contention was so sharp between them, that they departed asunder one from the other: and so Barnabas took Mark, and sailed unto Cyprus;

B. _____ JOHN MARK

2 TIMOTHY 4:11

11 Only Luke is with me. Take Mark, and bring him with thee: for he is profitable to me for the ministry.

Conclusion

_____

_____

_____

Study Questions

1. What does the name "Barnabas" mean?

2. List two areas in the life of Barnabas where he showed a willingness to give.

3. What former persecutor of Christians did Barnabas bring into the fellowship of the church?

4. To which outcast group of people did Barnabas minister?

5. What disgraced and rejected Christian brother did Barnabas restore to fellowship and usefulness?

6. List some specific ways in which you can act as a servant.

7. List some specific ways in which you can be an encouragement to others.

8. Specifically, what will you do to try to encourage someone this week?

Memory Verses

Who, when he came, and had seen the grace of God, was glad, and exhorted them all, that with purpose of heart they would cleave unto the Lord. For he was a good man, and full of the Holy Ghost and of faith: and much people was added unto the Lord.—ACTS 11:23–24

JOHN
The Beloved

Text

JOHN 13:21–25

21 When Jesus had thus said, he was troubled in spirit, and testified, and said, Verily, verily, I say unto you, that one of you shall betray me.

22 Then the disciples looked one on another, doubting of whom he spake.

23 Now there was leaning on Jesus' bosom one of his disciples, whom Jesus loved.

24 Simon Peter therefore beckoned to him, that he should ask who it should be of whom he spake.

25 He then lying on Jesus' breast saith unto him, Lord, who is it?

Overview

Of all the twelve disciples, Jesus had a special love for John. Wherever his Lord was, John tried to be as close as possible. After the ascension of Christ, John exhibited courage as one of the "pillars" of the early church. He was faithful to the Lord and was honored with the special vision of the Revelation of Jesus Christ.

Lesson Theme

While we know that the Lord Jesus Christ loves all of His children, there are qualities we can acquire and things we can do to draw even closer to Him. We can gain these qualities by learning from and emulating the life of John, the beloved disciple.

Introduction

_____

_____

_____

I. _____ of Christ

A. CLOSE IN _____

JOHN 13:23–26

23 **Now there was leaning on Jesus' bosom one of his disciples, whom Jesus loved.**

24 *Simon Peter therefore beckoned to him, that he should ask who it should be of whom he spake.*

25 *He then lying on Jesus' breast saith unto him, Lord, who is it?*

26 *Jesus answered, He it is, to whom I shall give a sop, when I have dipped it. And when he had dipped the sop, he gave it to Judas Iscariot, the son of Simon.*

B. CLOSE IN _____

JOHN 18:15–16

15 *And Simon Peter followed Jesus, **and so did another disciple**: that disciple was known unto the high priest, and went in with Jesus into the palace of the high priest.*

16 *But Peter stood at the door without. Then went out that other disciple, which was known unto the high priest, and spake unto her that kept the door, and brought in Peter.*

B. Close at the _____

John 19:26–27

26 When Jesus therefore saw his mother, **and the disciple standing by, whom he loved**, he saith unto his mother, Woman, behold thy son!

27 Then saith he to the disciple, Behold thy mother! And from that hour that disciple took her unto his own home.

II. _____ in Character

A. Stood against _____

2 John 7

7 For many deceivers are entered into the world, who confess not that Jesus Christ is come in the flesh. This is a deceiver and an antichrist.

B. Stood against _____

2 John 8

8 Look to yourselves, that we lose not those things which we have wrought, but that we receive a full reward.

III. _____ in Comparison

A. Faithful in _____

Revelation 1:9

9 I John, who also am your brother, and companion in tribulation, and in the kingdom and patience of Jesus Christ, was in the isle that is called Patmos, for the word of God, and for the testimony of Jesus Christ.

B. Faithful over _____

Conclusion

Study Questions

1. What special blessing did Elisha receive as a reward for staying close to his mentor Elijah?

2. List instances in the Gospels where it was apparent that John had an especially close relationship with Christ.

3. What motivated John to stand against those who stood against the Lord?

4. List some specific challenges that John gave the believers in his second epistle.

5. In what ways was John's life (after Christ went back to Heaven) different from the other disciples?

6. Where did John spend the later years of his life, and why was he there?

7. What special incident happened to John in that place?

8. In what specific ways can we imitate the life of John and understand more of what it means to be beloved of the Lord?

Memory Verse

And thou shalt love the Lord thy God with all thy heart, and with all thy soul, and with all thy mind, and with all thy strength: this is the first commandment.—MARK 12:30

JEREMIAH
Heart of Compassion

Text

JEREMIAH 4:14–19

14 O Jerusalem, wash thine heart from wickedness, that thou mayest be saved. How long shall thy vain thoughts lodge within thee?

15 For a voice declareth from Dan, and publisheth affliction from mount Ephraim.

16 Make ye mention to the nations; behold, publish against Jerusalem, that watchers come from a far country, and give out their voice against the cities of Judah.

17 As keepers of a field, are they against her round about; because she hath been rebellious against me, saith the LORD.

18 Thy way and thy doings have procured these things unto thee; this is thy wickedness, because it is bitter, because it reacheth unto thine heart.

19 My bowels, my bowels! I am pained at my very heart; my heart maketh a noise in me; I cannot hold my peace, because thou hast heard, O my soul, the sound of the trumpet, the alarm of war.

Overview

The Old Testament prophet Jeremiah cared so deeply for his people and was so pained by their wickedness that he has become known as the "Weeping Prophet." He had a fervent love for the lost and, although at one point in his life he almost quit the ministry, he could not keep himself from proclaiming the Word of God. He remained loyal to his Lord, faithfully preaching the message of God and His righteousness in spite of persecutions. He was able to do this because of his reliance on God's mercy and faithfulness.

Lesson Theme

Caring comes with a cost. In Jeremiah we see a faithful man of God who was willing to bear the burden of caring for a people who for the most part did not care. His example should inspire and instruct us in being the type of Christians God wants us to be and the type of Christians this world needs to see: a people who truly care in our hearts and in our actions.

Introduction

_____

_____

_____

PSALM 142:4

4   I looked on my right hand, and beheld, but there was no man that would know me: refuge failed me; no man cared for my soul.

I.   Love for the _____

A.   AFFECTED _____

JEREMIAH 4:18–19

18 Thy way and thy doings have procured these things unto thee; this is thy wickedness, because it is bitter, because it reacheth unto thine heart.

*19 **My bowels, my bowels! I am pained at my very heart; my heart maketh a noise in me;** I cannot hold my peace, because thou hast heard, O my soul, the sound of the trumpet, the alarm of war.*

MATTHEW 9:36

36 But when he [Christ] saw the multitudes, he was moved with compassion on them, because they fainted, and were scattered abroad, as sheep having no shepherd.

MATTHEW 6:22–23

22 The light of the body is the eye: if therefore thine eye be single, thy whole body shall be full of light.

23   But if thine eye be evil, thy whole body shall be full of darkness. If therefore the light that is in thee be darkness, how great is that darkness!

B. AFFECTED _____

JEREMIAH 20:9

9   Then I said, I will not make mention of him, nor speak any more in his name. But his word was in mine heart as a burning fire shut up in my bones, and I was weary with forbearing, and I could not stay.

II. Loyalty to the _____

A. IN HIS _____

JEREMIAH 42:4

4   Then Jeremiah the prophet said unto them, I have heard you; behold, I will pray unto the LORD your God according to your words; **and it shall come to pass, that whatsoever thing the LORD shall answer you, I will declare it unto you; I will keep nothing back from you.**

ACTS 20:27

27   For I have not shunned to declare unto you all the counsel of God.

1 CORINTHIANS 2:12–13

12   Now we have received, not the spirit of the world, but the spirit which is of God; that we might know the things that are freely given to us of God.
13   Which things also we speak, not in the words which man's wisdom teacheth, but which the Holy Ghost teacheth; comparing spiritual things with spiritual.

REVELATION 22:18–19

18 For I testify unto every man that heareth the words of the prophecy of this book, If any man shall add unto these things, God shall add unto him the plagues that are written in this book:

19 And if any man shall take away from the words of the book of this prophecy, God shall take away his part out of the book of life, and out of the holy city, and from the things which are written in this book.

B. IN HIS _____

JEREMIAH 38:6

6 Then took they Jeremiah, and cast him into the dungeon of Malchiah the son of Hammelech, that was in the court of the prison: and they let down Jeremiah with cords. And in the dungeon there was no water, but mire: so Jeremiah sunk in the mire.

III. Light of His _____

A. _____

LAMENTATIONS 3:21–22

21 This I recall to my mind, therefore have I hope.
22 It is of the LORD's mercies that we are not consumed, because his compassions fail not.

B. _____

LAMENTATIONS 3:23

*23 They are new every morning: **great is thy faithfulness.***

41

Conclusion

Study Questions

1. Why has Jeremiah become known as the "Weeping Prophet"?

2. God's Word teaches us that our eyes affect our hearts. What is meant by this?

3. Why did Jeremiah say that he could not keep from preaching the Word of God?

4. Describe one specific trial Jeremiah suffered because of his faithful stand for the Word of God.

5. What was the constant theme of Jeremiah's preaching?

6. How can we become more compassionate toward other people?

7. Are you living in such a way that the Lord would consider you a loyal Christian? In what areas do you need to become more loyal?

8. In what ways can you demonstrate mercy in your daily life?

Memory Verse

Oh that my head were waters, and mine eyes a fountain of tears, that I might weep day and night for the slain of the daughter of my people!—JEREMIAH 9:1

RUTH
From Defeat to Victory

Text

RUTH 1:19–22

19 So they two went until they came to Bethlehem. And it came to pass, when they were come to Bethlehem, that all the city was moved about them, and they said, Is this Naomi?

20 And she said unto them, Call me not Naomi, call me Mara: for the Almighty hath dealt very bitterly with me.

21 I went out full, and the LORD hath brought me home again empty: why then call ye me Naomi, seeing the LORD hath testified against me, and the Almighty hath afflicted me?

22 So Naomi returned, and Ruth the Moabitess, her daughter in law, with her, which returned out of the country of Moab: and they came to Bethlehem in the beginning of barley harvest.

Overview

Ruth knew both depths of sorrow and heights of blessing. From those depths, she followed her mother-in-law Naomi back to the land of the people of God. There she worked hard and faithfully, and God rewarded her with favor in the sight of Naomi's kinsman Boaz. They married, and Boaz and Ruth ultimately became the great-grandparents of King David and earthly ancestors of the Lord Jesus Christ.

Lesson Theme

Every one of us will face times of failure, defeat, temptations, and despair. It is important for us to realize that God never

45

forsakes His children, and no matter what the situation, there is always hope in the Lord. We need to follow godly direction and be faithful. In His own time, God will bring us to blessing and victory.

Introduction

_____

_____

_____

I. _____ in Following

1 Corinthians 4:2
2 Moreover it is required in stewards, that a man be found faithful.

Matthew 16:24
24 Then said Jesus unto his disciples, If any man will come after me, let him deny himself, and take up his cross, and follow me.

John 10:27
27 My sheep hear my voice, and I know them, and they follow me:

John 12:26
26 If any man serve me, let him follow me; and where I am, there shall also my servant be: if any man serve me, him will my Father honour.

A. **Followed Naomi's** _____

Ruth 1:22
*22 **So Naomi returned**, and Ruth the Moabitess, **her daughter in law, with her**, which returned out of the country of Moab: and they came to Bethlehem in the beginning of barley harvest.*

B. Followed Naomi's _____

PROVERBS 1:5

5   *A wise man will hear, and will increase learning;
and a man of understanding shall attain unto
wise counsels:*

1. **Go to Boaz's field.**

    RUTH 2:1–2

    *1   And Naomi had a kinsman of her husband's, a
    mighty man of wealth, of the family of Elimelech;
    and his name was Boaz.*
    *2   And Ruth the Moabitess said unto Naomi, Let
    me now go to the field, and glean ears of corn after
    him in whose sight I shall find grace.* **And she
    said unto her, Go, my daughter.**

2. **Go to Boaz's feet.**

    RUTH 3:6–7

    *6   And she went down unto the floor, and did
    according to all that her mother in law bade her.*
    *7   And when Boaz had eaten and drunk, and
    his heart was merry, he went to lie down at the
    end of the heap of corn:* **and she came softly, and
    uncovered his feet, and laid her down.**

    JOHN 1:41

    *41   He first findeth his own brother Simon, and
    saith unto him, We have found the Messias, which
    is, being interpreted, the Christ.*

    JOHN 1:45

    *45   Philip findeth Nathanael, and saith unto him,
    We have found him, of whom Moses in the law,*

and the prophets, did write, Jesus of Nazareth, the son of Joseph.

JOHN 4:29
29 *Come, see a man, which told me all things that ever I did: is not this the Christ?*

II. _____ in Laboring

A. _____ TO THE HARVEST

RUTH 2:3
3 **And she went, and came, and gleaned in the field after the reapers**: *and her hap was to light on a part of the field belonging unto Boaz, who was of the kindred of Elimelech.*

B. _____ IN THE HARVEST

RUTH 2:23
23 *So she kept fast by the maidens of Boaz to glean unto the end of barley harvest and of wheat harvest; and dwelt with her mother in law.*

LUKE 19:13
13 *And he called his ten servants, and delivered them ten pounds, and said unto them, Occupy till I come.*

III. _____ with Blessing

PROVERBS 28:20
20 *A faithful man shall abound with blessings...*

MATTHEW 6:24–33
24 *No man can serve two masters: for either he will hate the one, and love the other; or else he will hold to the one, and despise the other. Ye cannot serve God and mammon.*

25 Therefore I say unto you, Take no thought for your life, what ye shall eat, or what ye shall drink; nor yet for your body, what ye shall put on. Is not the life more than meat, and the body than raiment?

26 Behold the fowls of the air: for they sow not, neither do they reap, nor gather into barns; yet your heavenly Father feedeth them. Are ye not much better than they?

27 Which of you by taking thought can add one cubit unto his stature?

28 And why take ye thought for raiment? Consider the lilies of the field, how they grow; they toil not, neither do they spin:

29 And yet I say unto you, That even Solomon in all his glory was not arrayed like one of these.

30 Wherefore, if God so clothe the grass of the field, which to day is, and to morrow is cast into the oven, shall he not much more clothe you, O ye of little faith?

31 Therefore take no thought, saying, What shall we eat? or, What shall we drink? or, Wherewithal shall we be clothed?

32 (For after all these things do the Gentiles seek:) for your heavenly Father knoweth that ye have need of all these things.

33 But seek ye first the kingdom of God, and his righteousness; and all these things shall be added unto you.

JAMES 1:17

17 Every good gift and every perfect gift is from above, and cometh down from the Father of lights, with whom is no variableness, neither shadow of turning.

A. _____ NEEDS MET

RUTH 2:15–16

15 And when she was risen up to glean, Boaz commanded his young men, saying, Let her glean even among the sheaves, and reproach her not:

16 And let fall also some of the handfuls of purpose for her, and leave them, that she may glean them, and rebuke her not.

PSALM 37:25
25 I have been young, and now am old; yet have I not seen the righteous forsaken, nor his seed begging bread.

B. _____ NEEDS MET

RUTH 4:13
*13 **So Boaz took Ruth, and she was his wife:** and when he went in unto her, the LORD gave her conception, and she bare a son.*

Conclusion

_____

_____

_____

Study Questions

1. Where was Ruth's original home, and to where did she follow Naomi?

2. What did Ruth say to Naomi to express her willingness to follow?

3. When Naomi and Ruth returned to Bethlehem, where did Naomi send Ruth?

4. Explain the term "handfuls of purpose."

5. What does God promise us if we will seek first His kingdom and His righteousness?

6. What can you do to be a better worker—in your family, at your job, in your church?

7. What adversities are you facing today that tempt you to be discouraged?

8.   What Bible verses show you the way to overcome these adversities and find the way to victory?

Memory Verses

*And Ruth said, Intreat me not to leave thee, or to return from following after thee: for whither thou goest, I will go; and where thou lodgest, I will lodge: thy people shall be my people, and thy God my God: Where thou diest, will I die, and there will I be buried: the LORD do so to me, and more also, if ought but death part thee and me.—*RUTH 1:16–17

JOB
Trusting in Tribulations

Text

JOB 23:8–12

8 *Behold, I go forward, but he is not there; and backward, but I cannot perceive him:*

9 *On the left hand, where he doth work, but I cannot behold him: he hideth himself on the right hand, that I cannot see him:*

10 *But he knoweth the way that I take: when he hath tried me, I shall come forth as gold.*

11 *My foot hath held his steps, his way have I kept, and not declined.*

12 *Neither have I gone back from the commandment of his lips; I have esteemed the words of his mouth more than my necessary food.*

Overview

By all earthly standards, Job was a good man. Even God pointed him out to Satan as someone special. In this lesson we will see why and how the severest of trials came to Job, and how after a period of suffering and questioning, Job was eventually exalted by God when he humbled himself.

Lesson Theme

All of us have wondered at times why we suffer and why others suffer. God has a purpose in permitting trials to come into our lives. If our lives were always smooth and everything were easy, we would never grow much in our faith. Learning to trust God through our trials leads to triumph.

Introduction

_____

_____

_____

I. _____

A. _____ AND _____

JOB 1:1

1   *There was a man in the land of Uz, whose name was Job; and that man was perfect and upright,* and one that feared God, and eschewed evil.

B. _____ GOD

JOB 1:1

1   *There was a man in the land of Uz, whose name was Job; and that man was perfect and upright,* **and one that feared God,** *and eschewed evil.*

C. ESCHEWED _____

JOB 1:1

1   *There was a man in the land of Uz, whose name was Job; and that man was perfect and upright, and one that feared God,* **and eschewed evil.**

PSALM 97:10

10   *Ye that love the LORD, hate evil: he preserveth the souls of his saints; he delivereth them out of the hand of the wicked.*

HEBREWS 1:9

9   *Thou hast loved righteousness, and hated iniquity; therefore God, even thy God, hath anointed thee with the oil of gladness above thy fellows.*

1 JOHN 2:15–17

15   *Love not the world, neither the things that are in the world. If any man love the world, the love of the Father is not in him.*

16   *For all that is in the world, the lust of the flesh, and the lust of the eyes, and the pride of life, is not of the Father, but is of the world.*

17   *And the world passeth away, and the lust thereof: but he that doeth the will of God abideth for ever.*

II. _____

A. _____ TRIALS

JOB 1:13–17

13   *And there was a day when his sons and his daughters were eating and drinking wine in their eldest brother's house:*

14   *And there came a messenger unto Job, and said, The oxen were plowing, and the asses feeding beside them:*

15   *And the Sabeans fell upon them, and took them away; yea, they have slain the servants with the edge of the sword; and I only am escaped alone to tell thee.*

16   *While he was yet speaking, there came also another, and said, The fire of God is fallen from heaven, and hath burned up the sheep, and the servants, and consumed them; and I only am escaped alone to tell thee.*

17 While he was yet speaking, there came also another, and said, The Chaldeans made out three bands, and fell upon the camels, and have carried them away, yea, and slain the servants with the edge of the sword; and I only am escaped alone to tell thee.

B. _____ TRIALS

JOB 1:18–19

18 While he was yet speaking, there came also another, and said, Thy sons and thy daughters were eating and drinking wine in their eldest brother's house:

19 And, behold, there came a great wind from the wilderness, and smote the four corners of the house, and it fell upon the young men, and they are dead; and I only am escaped alone to tell thee.

C. _____ TRIALS

JOB 2:7–10

7 So went Satan forth from the presence of the LORD, and smote Job with sore boils from the sole of his foot unto his crown.

8 And he took him a potsherd to scrape himself withal; and he sat down among the ashes.

9 Then said his wife unto him, Dost thou still retain thine integrity? curse God, and die.

10 But he said unto her, Thou speakest as one of the foolish women speaketh. What? shall we receive good at the hand of God, and shall we not receive evil? In all this did not Job sin with his lips.

III. _____

A. _____

JOB 42:1–6

1   Then Job answered the LORD, and said,

2   I know that thou canst do every thing, and that no thought can be withholden from thee.

3   Who is he that hideth counsel without knowledge? therefore have I uttered that I understood not; things too wonderful for me, which I knew not.

4   Hear, I beseech thee, and I will speak: I will demand of thee, and declare thou unto me.

5   I have heard of thee by the hearing of the ear: but now mine eye seeth thee.

6   Wherefore I abhor myself, and repent in dust and ashes.

PROVERBS 6:23

23   For the commandment is a lamp; and the law is light; and reproofs of instruction are the way of life:

B. _____

JOB 42:12–13

12   So the LORD blessed the latter end of Job more than his beginning: for he had fourteen thousand sheep, and six thousand camels, and a thousand yoke of oxen, and a thousand she asses.

13   He had also seven sons and three daughters.

Conclusion

_____

_____

_____

Study Questions

1. How did God describe Job to Satan?

2. Through the workings of Satan, what did Job lose?

3. What did Job say after he had lost his property and his children?

4. What has been an example of a great loss in your life, and how did you deal with it?

5. Looking back on this great loss now, do you believe you could you have dealt with it better? How?

6. How can we gain wisdom through our trials?

7. In what two ways did Job triumph through his trials?

8. What have you learned from the story of Job that will help you the next time you face a trial?

Memory Verses

There was a man in the land of Uz, whose name was Job; and that man was perfect and upright, and one that feared God, and eschewed evil.—JOB 1:1

Then Job arose, and rent his mantle, and shaved his head, and fell down upon the ground, and worshipped, And said, Naked came I out of my mother's womb, and naked shall I return thither: the LORD gave, and the LORD hath taken away; blessed be the name of the LORD.—JOB 1:20–21

SAMSON
Wasted Potential

Text

JUDGES 16:16–20

16 And it came to pass, when she pressed him daily with her words, and urged him, so that his soul was vexed unto death;

17 That he told her all his heart, and said unto her. There hath not come a razor upon mine head; for I have been a Nazarite unto God from my mother's womb: if I be shaven, then my strength will go from me, and I shall become weak, and be like any other man.

18 And when Delilah saw that he had told her all his heart, she sent and called for the lords of the Philistines, saying, Come up this once, for he hath shewed me all his heart. Then the lords of the Philistines came up unto her, and brought money in their hand.

19 And she made him sleep upon her knees; and she called for a man, and she caused him to shave off the seven locks of his head; and she began to afflict him, and his strength went from him.

20 And she said, The Philistines be upon thee, Samson. And he awoke out of his sleep, and said, I will go out as at other times before, and shake myself. And he wist not that the LORD was departed from him.

Overview

Samson—though born of an answer to prayer, dedicated to God by his parents, and destined to be a deliverer of his people—lived his life in a prideful pleasure-seeking way that led to a shameful and tragic end. It began in his heart, manifested itself in disobedience to his parents and to God, continued as he allowed his fleshly desires to rule over him, and finally culminated in captivity, blindness, and death.

Lesson Theme

No matter how strong and good-looking one may be physically, if the heart is not right with God, the inevitable result will be failure. The greatest waste of all may very well be the waste of potential for God.

Introduction

_____

_____

_____

I. Samson _____

A. To his _____

JUDGES 14:3

3   Then his father and his mother said unto him, Is there never a woman among the daughters of thy brethren, or among all my people, that thou goest to take a wife of the uncircumcised Philistines? And Samson said unto his father, Get her for me; for she pleaseth me well.

EXODUS 20:12

12   Honour thy father and thy mother: that thy days may be long upon the land which the LORD thy God giveth thee.

EPHESIANS 6:1

1   Children, obey your parents in the Lord: for this is right.

COLOSSIANS 3:20

20   Children, obey your parents in all things: for this is well pleasing unto the Lord.

B. To his _____

JUDGES 13:3–5

3   And the angel of the LORD appeared unto the woman, and said unto her, Behold now, thou art barren, and bearest not: but thou shalt conceive, and bear a son.

4   Now therefore beware, I pray thee, and drink not wine nor strong drink, and eat not any unclean thing:
5   For, lo, thou shalt conceive, and bear a son; and no razor shall come on his head: for the child shall be a Nazarite unto God from the womb: and he shall begin to deliver Israel out of the hand of the Philistines.

NUMBERS 6:6

6   All the days that he [the Nazarite] separateth himself unto the LORD he shall come at no dead body.

JUDGES 14:8–9

8   And after a time he returned to take her, and he turned aside to see the carcase of the lion: and, behold, there was a swarm of bees and honey in the carcase of the lion.
9   And he took thereof in his hands, and went on eating, and came to his father and mother, and he gave them, and they did eat: but he told not them that he had taken the honey out of the carcase of the lion.

DEUTERONOMY 23:21

21   When thou shalt vow a vow unto the LORD thy God, thou shalt not slack to pay it: for the LORD thy God will surely require it of thee; and it would be sin in thee.

1 JOHN 2:15–17

15   Love not the world, neither the things that are in the world. If any man love the world, the love of the Father is not in him.
16   For all that is in the world, the lust of the flesh, and the lust of the eyes, and the pride of life, is not of the Father, but is of the world.

17 And the world passeth away, and the lust thereof: but he that doeth the will of God abideth for ever.

ROMANS 8:12

12 Therefore, brethren, we are debtors, not to the flesh, to live after the flesh.

JAMES 1:14–15

14 But every man is tempted, when he is drawn away of his own lust, and enticed.

15 Then when lust hath conceived, it bringeth forth sin: and sin, when it is finished, bringeth forth death.

II. Samson

PHILIPPIANS 3:13–14

13 Brethren, I count not myself to have apprehended: but this one thing I do, forgetting those things which are behind, and reaching forth unto those things which are before,

14 I press toward the mark for the prize of the high calling of God in Christ Jesus.

HEBREWS 12:1–2

1 Wherefore seeing we also are compassed about with so great a cloud of witnesses, let us lay aside every weight, and the sin which doth so easily beset us, and let us run with patience the race that is set before us,

2 Looking unto Jesus the author and finisher of our faith; who for the joy that was set before him endured the cross, despising the shame, and is set down at the right hand of the throne of God.

1 CORINTHIANS 9:25–27

25 And every man that striveth for the mastery is temperate in all things. Now they do it to obtain a corruptible crown; but we an incorruptible.

26 I therefore so run, not as uncertainly; so fight I, not as one that beateth the air:

27 But I keep under my body, and bring it into subjection: lest that by any means, when I have preached to others, I myself should be a castaway.

    A. _____ VICTORIES

    B. _____ TEMPTATIONS

III.   Samson _____

    A. DEPLETION OF _____

       JUDGES 16:20

       20 And she said, The Philistines be upon thee, Samson. And he awoke out of his sleep, and said, I will go out as at other times before, and shake myself. And he wist not that the LORD was departed from him.

       ISAIAH 59:1–2

       1 Behold, the LORD's hand is not shortened, that it cannot save; neither his ear heavy, that it cannot hear:

       2 But your iniquities have separated between you and your God, and your sins have hid his face from you, that he will not hear.

    B. DEVASTATION OF _____

Conclusion

_____

_____

_____

Study Questions

1. Give examples of Samson's disobedience.

2. Give some examples of Bible verses that guide us in the attitude we should have toward our parents.

3. What attitudes in Samson's heart led him to disobey his parents and his God?

4. In general, on what do God's people need to focus?

5. Why did Samson say he wanted Delilah?

6. In what area or areas of your life is your focus on pleasing yourself rather than pleasing God?

7. What did Dr. Bob Jones, Sr. mean when he said, "Don't sacrifice the permanent on the altar of the immediate"?

8.   What effect does our sin have on our relationship with God?

Memory Verse

And she said, The Philistines be upon thee, Samson. And he awoke out of his sleep, and said, I will go out as at other times before, and shake myself. And he wist not that the LORD was departed from him.—JUDGES 16:20

CENTURION
The Man Who Amazed Jesus

Text

LUKE 7:6–9

6 *Then Jesus went with them. And when he was now not far from the house, the centurion sent friends to him, saying unto him, Lord, trouble not thyself: for I am not worthy that thou shouldest enter under my roof:*

7 *Wherefore neither thought I myself worthy to come unto thee: but say in a word, and my servant shall be healed.*

8 *For I also am a man set under authority, having under me soldiers, and I say unto one, Go, and he goeth; and to another, Come, and he cometh; and to my servant, Do this, and he doeth it.*

9 *When Jesus heard these things, he marvelled at him, and turned him about, and said unto the people that followed him, I say unto you, I have not found so great faith, no, not in Israel.*

Overview

Of all the people Jesus encountered during His time here on the earth, only a few really impressed Him. One of these was a Roman centurion who displayed such generosity, humility, and faith that the Bible says Jesus "marvelled." In our lesson today, we will take a closer look at each of these qualities, see how this centurion exemplified them, and learn how we can cultivate these traits in our own lives.

Lesson Theme

God's generosity to us should encourage us to be a giving people. God's greatness should prompt us to humility and a realization of our own unworthiness. God's trustworthiness should lead us to a life of walking by faith.

Introduction

_____

_____

_____

I. Great _____

A. GENEROSITY TO HIS _____

LUKE 7:2

2   And a certain centurion's servant, who was dear unto him, was sick, and ready to die.

1 THESSALONIANS 5:14

14   Now we exhort you, brethren, warn them that are unruly, comfort the feebleminded, support the weak, be patient toward all men.

ROMANS 15:1

1   We then that are strong ought to bear the infirmities of the weak, and not to please ourselves.

EPHESIANS 4:32

32   And be ye kind one to another, tenderhearted, forgiving one another, even as God for Christ's sake hath forgiven you.

LUKE 6:35

35   But love ye your enemies, and do good, and lend, hoping for nothing again; and your reward shall be great, and ye shall be the children of the Highest: for he is kind unto the unthankful and to the evil.

B. GENEROSITY TO THE _____

LUKE 7:5

5   *For he loveth our nation, and he hath built us a synagogue.*

II. Great _____

JAMES 4:6

6   *But he giveth more grace. Wherefore he saith, God resisteth the proud, but giveth grace unto the humble.*

1 PETER 5:5

5   *Likewise, ye younger, submit yourselves unto the elder. Yea, all of you be subject one to another, and be clothed with humility: for God resisteth the proud, and giveth grace to the humble.*

A. NOT WORTHY TO COME TO _____

LUKE 7:3

3   *And when he heard of Jesus, he sent unto him the elders of the Jews, beseeching him that he would come and heal his servant.*

LUKE 7:7

7   *Wherefore neither thought I myself worthy to come unto thee: but say in a word, and my servant shall be healed.*

HEBREWS 4:16

16   *Let us therefore come boldly unto the throne of grace, that we may obtain mercy, and find grace to help in time of need.*

B. **NOT WORTHY FOR JESUS TO COME TO** _____

LUKE 7:6–7

6   Then Jesus went with them. And when he was now not far from the house, the centurion sent friends to him, saying unto him, Lord, trouble not thyself: for I am not worthy that thou shouldest enter under my roof:

7   Wherefore neither thought I myself worthy to come unto thee…

MATTHEW 28:18

18   And Jesus came and spake unto them, saying, All power is given unto me in heaven and in earth.

JOHN 6:6

6   And this he said to prove him: for he himself knew what he would do.

LAMENTATIONS 3:22

22   It is of the LORD's mercies that we are not consumed, because his compassions fail not.

EPHESIANS 2:8–9

8   For by grace are ye saved through faith; and that not of yourselves: it is the gift of God:

9   Not of works, lest any man should boast.

III. Great _____

HEBREWS 11:1–2

1   Now faith is the substance of things hoped for, the evidence of things not seen.

2   For by it the elders obtained a good report.

ROMANS 14:23

23   …whatsoever is not of faith is sin.

2 Corinthians 5:7

7   *(For we walk by faith, not by sight:)*

Hebrews 11:6

6   *But without faith it is impossible to please him: for he that cometh to God must believe that he is, and that he is a rewarder of them that diligently seek him.*

A. Great faith _____

Luke 7:7

7   *Wherefore neither thought I myself worthy to come unto thee: but say in a word, and my servant shall be healed.*

Genesis 1:1–3, 6, 9, 11

1   *In the beginning God created the heaven and the earth.*

2   *And the earth was without form, and void; and darkness was upon the face of the deep. And the Spirit of God moved upon the face of the waters.*

3   **And God said**, *Let there be light: and there was light.*

6   **And God said**, *Let there be a firmament in the midst of the waters, and let it divide the waters from the waters.*

9   **And God said**, *Let the waters under the heaven be gathered together unto one place, and let the dry land appear: and it was so.*

11   **And God said**, *Let the earth bring forth grass, the herb yielding seed, and the fruit tree yielding fruit after his kind, whose seed is in itself, upon the earth: and it was so.*

JOHN 1:1–3

1   In the beginning was the Word, and the Word was with God, and the Word was God.

2   The same was in the beginning with God.

3   All things were made by him; and without him was not any thing made that was made.

EXODUS 31:18

18   And he gave unto Moses, when he had made an end of communing with him upon mount Sinai, two tables of testimony, tables of stone, written with the finger of God.

HEBREWS 4:12

12   For the word of God is quick, and powerful, and sharper than any twoedged sword, piercing even to the dividing asunder of soul and spirit, and of the joints and marrow, and is a discerner of the thoughts and intents of the heart.

B. GREAT FAITH _____

LUKE 7:9

9   When Jesus heard these things, he marvelled at him, and turned him about, and said unto the people that followed him, I say unto you, I have not found so great faith, no, not in Israel.

Conclusion

_____

_____

_____

Study Questions

1. What three major characteristics of the centurion did we study in this lesson?

2. In what ways did the centurion demonstrate his generosity?

3. In what ways did the centurion demonstrate his humility?

4. Complete this sentence: "Without _____, it is impossible to please God." What verse tells us this?

5. How did the centurion demonstrate his faith?

6. In what specific ways can you show a spirit of generosity this week?

7. In what specific ways can you show a spirit of humility this week?

8.   In what specific ways can you demonstrate faith this week: not merely believing, but acting upon the belief?

Memory Verse

When Jesus heard these things, he marvelled at him, and turned him about, and said unto the people that followed him, I say unto you, I have not found so great faith, no, not in Israel.—LUKE 7:9

ESTHER
Found Faithful

Text

ESTHER 4:13–17

13 Then Mordecai commanded to answer Esther, Think not with thyself that thou shalt escape in the king's house, more than all the Jews.

14 For if thou altogether holdest thy peace at this time, then shall there enlargement and deliverance arise to the Jews from another place; but thou and thy father's house shall be destroyed: and who knoweth whether thou art come to the kingdom for such a time as this?

15 Then Esther bade them return Mordecai this answer,

16 Go, gather together all the Jews that are present in Shushan, and fast ye for me, and neither eat nor drink three days, night or day: I also and my maidens will fast likewise; and so will I go in unto the king, which is not according to the law: and if I perish, I perish.

17 So Mordecai went his way, and did according to all that Esther had commanded him.

Overview

Through the malicious workings of a jealous and wicked man, God's people found themselves in great danger. But God in His providence had already placed a special young lady in a key position. Queen Esther courageously trusted in the Lord and interceded for her people, and God worked a great miracle of deliverance.

Lesson Theme

"For such a time as this," God had a vital place and a special task for a prepared person. We may not know why God has put us where we are, but we can be assured that God has a good reason. Our responsibility is, as was Esther's, to be prepared and submissive to God so that He can use us as He desires.

Introduction

_____

_____

_____

I. _____ Times

A. UNCERTAIN _____

ESTHER 3:8–9

8   And Haman said unto king Ahasuerus, There is a certain people scattered abroad and dispersed among the people in all the provinces of thy kingdom; and their laws are diverse from all people; neither keep they the king's laws: therefore it is not for the king's profit to suffer them.

9   **If it please the king, let it be written that they may be destroyed**: and I will pay ten thousand talents of silver to the hands of those that have the charge of the business, to bring it into the king's treasuries.

B. UNAPPROACHABLE _____

ESTHER 4:11

11   **All the king's servants, and the people of the king's provinces, do know, that whosoever, whether man or woman, shall come unto the king into the inner court, who is not called, there is one law of his to put him to death,** except such to whom the king shall hold out the golden sceptre, that he may live: but I have not been called to come in unto the king these thirty days.

II. _____ **Traits**

A. CARED ENOUGH TO _____

ESTHER 4:14

14 For if thou altogether holdest thy peace at this time, then shall there enlargement and deliverance arise to the Jews from another place; but thou and thy father's house shall be destroyed: and who knoweth whether thou art come to the kingdom for such a time as this?

ESTHER 8:3

3 And Esther spake yet again before the king, and fell down at his feet, and besought him with tears to put away the mischief of Haman the Agagite, and his device that he had devised against the Jews.

B. CARED ENOUGH TO _____ AND _____

ESTHER 4:16

16 Go, gather together all the Jews that are present in Shushan, and fast ye for me, and neither eat nor drink three days, night or day: I also and my maidens will fast likewise; and so will I go in unto the king, which is not according to the law: and if I perish, I perish.

MARK 9:25–29

25 When Jesus saw that the people came running together, he rebuked the foul spirit, saying unto him, Thou dumb and deaf spirit, I charge thee, come out of him, and enter no more into him.

26 And the spirit cried, and rent him sore, and came out of him: and he was as one dead; insomuch that many said, He is dead.

27 But Jesus took him by the hand, and lifted him up; and he arose.

28 And when he was come into the house, his disciples asked him privately, Why could not we cast him out?

29 And he said unto them, This kind can come forth by nothing, but by prayer and fasting.

III. _____ **Testimony**

A. _____

ESTHER 8:4

4 Then the king held out the golden sceptre toward Esther. So Esther arose, and stood before the king,

ESTHER 7:10

10 So they hanged Haman on the gallows that he had prepared for Mordecai. Then was the king's wrath pacified.

B. _____

ESTHER 8:2

2 And the king took off his ring, which he had taken from Haman, and gave it unto Mordecai. And Esther set Mordecai over the house of Haman.

ESTHER 8:15

15 And Mordecai went out from the presence of the king in royal apparel of blue and white, and with a great crown of gold, and with a garment of fine linen and purple: and the city of Shushan rejoiced and was glad.

C. _____

ESTHER 8:16–17

16 The Jews had light, and gladness, and joy, and honour.

17 And in every province, and in every city, whithersoever the king's commandment and his decree came, the Jews had joy and gladness, a feast and a good day. And many of the people of the land became Jews; for the fear of the Jews fell upon them.

Conclusion

Study Questions

1. What was Haman's plot?

2. Unless the king granted special mercy, what would happen to someone who came to the king uninvited?

3. Who was Esther's spiritual mentor?

4. What three actions did Esther take in attempting to get the decree against her people reversed?

5. Describe the end of Haman.

6. How can you exercise boldness for God this week?

7. For what special problems in your life would you be willing to fast and pray for a solution?

8. Describe a time in your life when God gave you a remarkable or even a miraculous deliverance.

Memory Verses

*Then Mordecai commanded to answer Esther, Think not with thyself that thou shalt escape in the king's house, more than all the Jews. For if thou altogether holdest thy peace at this time, then shall there enlargement and deliverance arise to the Jews from another place; but thou and thy father's house shall be destroyed: and who knoweth whether thou art come to the kingdom for such a time as this?—*ESTHER 4:13–14

ELISHA
A Double Portion

Text

2 KINGS 2:8–14

8   *And Elijah took his mantle, and wrapped it together, and smote the waters, and they were divided hither and thither, so that they two went over on dry ground.*

9   *And it came to pass, when they were gone over, that Elijah said unto Elisha, Ask what I shall do for thee, before I be taken away from thee. And Elisha said, I pray thee, let a double portion of thy spirit be upon me.*

10   *And he said, Thou hast asked a hard thing: nevertheless, if thou see me when I am taken from thee, it shall be so unto thee; but if not, it shall not be so.*

11   *And it came to pass, as they still went on, and talked, that, behold, there appeared a chariot of fire, and horses of fire, and parted them both asunder; and Elijah went up by a whirlwind into heaven.*

12   *And Elisha saw it, and he cried, My father, my father, the chariot of Israel, and the horsemen thereof. And he saw him no more: and he took hold of his own clothes, and rent them in two pieces.*

13   *He took up also the mantle of Elijah that fell from him, and went back, and stood by the bank of Jordan;*

14   *And he took the mantle of Elijah that fell from him, and smote the waters, and said, Where is the* LORD *God of Elijah? and when he also had smitten the waters, they parted hither and thither: and Elisha went over.*

Overview

Elisha was just a simple farm boy who was out in the field plowing when a prophet named Elijah came by and chose him as a protégé and successor. Elisha left the farm and followed the man of God. When the time came for Elijah to leave this world, Elisha was ready and bold enough to ask for a double portion of the spirit that Elijah had. God granted his request, and the power that rested on Elisha was obvious to everyone around him.

Lesson Theme

Elisha showed faithfulness first in his own home and then in the work of God. Elisha showed fervency as he followed God's man and stuck with him to the end. Elisha showed fearlessness as he refused to turn back to the old life and carried on for God, bolstered by a double portion of power. Faithfulness, fervency, fearlessness—a mighty combination that God can use in a wonderful way!

Introduction

_____

_____

_____

I. _____

1 Kings 19:19

_19 So he_ [Elijah] _departed thence, and found Elisha the son of Shaphat, who was plowing with twelve yoke of oxen before him, and he with the twelfth: and Elijah passed by him, and cast his mantle upon him._

Proverbs 20:6

6 Most men will proclaim every one his own goodness: but a faithful man who can find?

Luke 16:10

10 He that is faithful in that which is least is faithful also in much: and he that is unjust in the least is unjust also in much.

A. Faithful in his _____

B. Faithful to his _____
1 Kings 19:19–21

19 So he departed thence, and found Elisha the son of Shaphat, who was plowing with twelve yoke of oxen before him, and he with the twelfth: and Elijah passed by him, and cast his mantle upon him.

20 And he left the oxen, and ran after Elijah, and said, Let me, I pray thee, kiss my father and my mother, and then I will follow thee. And he said unto him, Go back again: for what have I done to thee?

21 And he returned back from him, and took a yoke of oxen, and slew them, and boiled their flesh with the instruments of the oxen, and gave unto the people, and they did eat. Then he arose, and went after Elijah, and ministered unto him.

II. _____

A. FERVENT TO _____ THE CALL

1 KINGS 19:20

20 And he left the oxen, and ran after Elijah, and said, Let me, I pray thee, kiss my father and my mother, and then I will follow thee. And he said unto him, Go back again: for what have I done to thee?

B. FERVENT TO REMAIN _____ IN SERVICE

2 KINGS 2:2–6

2 And Elijah said unto Elisha, Tarry here, I pray thee; for the LORD hath sent me to Bethel. **And Elisha said unto him, As the LORD liveth, and as thy soul liveth, I will not leave thee.** *So they went down to Bethel.*

3 And the sons of the prophets that were at Bethel came forth to Elisha, and said unto him, Knowest thou that the LORD will take away thy master from thy head to day? And he said, Yea, I know it; hold ye your peace.

4 And Elijah said unto him, Elisha, tarry here, I pray thee; for the LORD hath sent me to Jericho. **And he said, As the LORD liveth, and as thy soul liveth, I will not leave thee.** *So they came to Jericho.*

5 And the sons of the prophets that were at Jericho came to Elisha, and said unto him, Knowest thou that the LORD will take away thy master from thy head to day? And he answered, Yea, I know it; hold ye your peace.

6   And Elijah said unto him, Tarry, I pray thee, here; for the Lord *hath sent me to Jordan.* **And he said, As the LORD liveth, and as thy soul liveth, I will not leave thee.** *And they two went on.*

Amos 3:3

3   Can two walk together, except they be agreed?

Proverbs 27:17

17   Iron sharpeneth iron; so a man sharpeneth the countenance of his friend.

1 Samuel 23:16

16   And Jonathan Saul's son arose, and went to David into the wood, and strengthened his hand in God.

III.

A. Fearless _____

1 Kings 19:20–21

20   And he left the oxen, and ran after Elijah, and said, Let me, I pray thee, kiss my father and my mother, and then I will follow thee. And he said unto him, Go back again: for what have I done to thee?

21   And he returned back from him, and took a yoke of oxen, and slew them, and boiled their flesh with the instruments of the oxen, and gave unto the people, and they did eat. Then he arose, and went after Elijah, and ministered unto him.

Hebrews 12:1

1   Wherefore seeing we also are compassed about with so great a cloud of witnesses, let us lay aside every weight, and the sin which doth so easily beset us, and let us run with patience the race that is set before us,

1 TIMOTHY 6:7
7   *For we brought nothing into this world, and it is certain we can carry nothing out.*

B. FEARLESS _____
2 KINGS 2:9
9   *And it came to pass, when they were gone over, that Elijah said unto Elisha, Ask what I shall do for thee, before I be taken away from thee. And Elisha said, I pray thee, let a double portion of thy spirit be upon me.*

C. FEARLESS _____
2 KINGS 2:13–15
13   *He took up also the mantle of Elijah that fell from him, and went back, and stood by the bank of Jordan;*
14   *And he took the mantle of Elijah that fell from him, and smote the waters, and said, Where is the LORD God of Elijah? and when he also had smitten the waters, they parted hither and thither: and Elisha went over.*
15   *And when the sons of the prophets which were to view at Jericho saw him, they said, The spirit of Elijah doth rest on Elisha. And they came to meet him, and bowed themselves to the ground before him.*

Conclusion

Study Questions

1. How did Elisha signify his decision to follow the man of God?

2. How did Elisha show his fervency and eagerness to follow the man of God?

3. What are some things that you have left behind for the Lord?

4. When Elijah asked Elisha what he should do for him before he left, what was Elisha's answer?

5. How did Elisha demonstrate his new power from God?

6. In what areas of your life do you need to demonstrate more faithfulness?

7. In what areas of your life do you need to demonstrate more fervency?

8. In what areas of your life do you need to demonstrate more fearlessness?

Memory Verses

He took up also the mantle of Elijah that fell from him, and went back, and stood by the bank of Jordan; And he took the mantle of Elijah that fell from him, and smote the waters, and said, Where is the LORD God of Elijah? and when he also had smitten the waters, they parted hither and thither: and Elisha went over.

—2 KINGS 2:13–14

JOSEPH
Living Like Jesus

Text

GENESIS 50:17–21

17 So shall ye say unto Joseph, Forgive, I pray thee now, the trespass of thy brethren, and their sin; for they did unto thee evil: and now, we pray thee, forgive the trespass of the servants of the God of thy father. And Joseph wept when they spake unto him.

18 And his brethren also went and fell down before his face; and they said, Behold, we be thy servants.

19 And Joseph said unto them, Fear not: for am I in the place of God?

20 But as for you, ye thought evil against me; but God meant it unto good, to bring to pass, as it is this day, to save much people alive.

21 Now therefore fear ye not: I will nourish you, and your little ones. And he comforted them, and spake kindly unto them.

Overview

Joseph played a pivotal role in the history of the Hebrew people. Through many circumstances that were certainly not comfortable for him, God brought Joseph from the status of a favored son, through slavery and unjust imprisonment, to a place of prominence in a foreign country. When famine came to the land of Canaan, Joseph in Egypt became the savior of his family.

Lesson Theme

All of us face discouraging circumstances in our lives. The important thing is not so much what happens to us, but rather how we deal with them. In Joseph we see a wonderful example of a man who remained faithful through his trials and was rewarded by God with great usefulness and blessing.

Introduction

_____

_____

I.   Faithful as a _____

A.   _____ BY HIS _____

GENESIS 37:3

3   Now Israel loved Joseph more than all his children, because he was the son of his old age: and he made him a coat of many colours.

B.   _____ BY HIS _____

GENESIS 37:4

4   And when his brethren saw that their father loved him more than all his brethren, they hated him, and could not speak peaceably unto him.

C.   _____ TO HIS _____

GENESIS 37:14

14   And he [Joseph's father Israel] said to him, Go, I pray thee, see whether it be well with thy brethren, and well with the flocks; and bring me word again. So he sent him out of the vale of Hebron, and he came to Shechem.

II. Faithful as a _____

MATTHEW 23:11

11   But he that is greatest among you shall be your servant.

A. POTIPHAR'S _____

GENESIS 39:4
4   And Joseph found grace in his sight, and he served him: and he made him overseer over his house, and all that he had he put into his hand.

PROVERBS 22:1
1   A good name is rather to be chosen than great riches, and loving favour rather than silver and gold.

B. PHARAOH'S _____

GENESIS 39:21–22
21   But the LORD was with Joseph, and shewed him mercy, and gave him favour in the sight of the keeper of the prison. 22   And the keeper of the prison committed to Joseph's hand all the prisoners that were in the prison; and whatsoever they did there, he was the doer of it.

ROMANS 8:35
35   Who shall separate us from the love of Christ? shall tribulation, or distress, or persecution, or famine, or nakedness, or peril, or sword?

2 TIMOTHY 3:12
12   Yea, and all that will live godly in Christ Jesus shall suffer persecution.

JOHN 16:33
33   These things I have spoken unto you, that in me ye might have peace. In the world ye shall have tribulation: but be of good cheer; I have overcome the world.

C. PEOPLE OF _____

GENESIS 41:38–44
38   And Pharaoh said unto his servants, Can we find such a one as this is, a man in whom the Spirit of God is?

39 And Pharaoh said unto Joseph, Forasmuch as God hath shewed thee all this, there is none so discreet and wise as thou art:

40 Thou shalt be over my house, and according unto thy word shall all my people be ruled: only in the throne will I be greater than thou.

41 And Pharaoh said unto Joseph, See, I have set thee over all the land of Egypt.

42 And Pharaoh took off his ring from his hand, and put it upon Joseph's hand, and arrayed him in vestures of fine linen, and put a gold chain about his neck;

43 And he made him to ride in the second chariot which he had; and they cried before him, Bow the knee: and he made him ruler over all the land of Egypt.

44 And Pharaoh said unto Joseph, I am Pharaoh, and without thee shall no man lift up his hand or foot in all the land of Egypt.

PSALM 27:14

14 Wait on the LORD: be of good courage, and he shall strengthen thine heart: wait, I say, on the LORD.

III. Faithful as a _____

A. _____ SOVEREIGN

GENESIS 50:17–21

17 So shall ye say unto Joseph, Forgive, I pray thee now, the trespass of thy brethren, and their sin; for they did unto thee evil: and now, we pray thee, forgive the trespass of the servants of the God of thy father. And Joseph wept when they spake unto him.

18 And his brethren also went and fell down before his face; and they said, Behold, we be thy servants.

19 And Joseph said unto them, Fear not: for am I in the place of God?

20 But as for you, ye thought evil against me; but God meant it unto good, to bring to pass, as it is this day, to save much people alive.

21 Now therefore fear ye not: I will nourish you, and your little ones. And he comforted them, and spake kindly unto them.

ROMANS 5:8–10

8 But God commendeth his love toward us, in that, while we were yet sinners, Christ died for us.

9 Much more then, being now justified by his blood, we shall be saved from wrath through him.

10 For if, when we were enemies, we were reconciled to God by the death of his Son, much more, being reconciled, we shall be saved by his life.

EPHESIANS 4:32

32 And be ye kind one to another, tenderhearted, forgiving one another, even as God for Christ's sake hath forgiven you.

ROMANS 12:19

19 Dearly beloved, avenge not yourselves, but rather give place unto wrath: for it is written, Vengeance is mine; I will repay, saith the Lord.

B. _____ SOVEREIGN

GENESIS 50:20

20 But as for you, ye thought evil against me; but God meant it unto good, to bring to pass, as it is this day, to save much people alive.

Conclusion

Study Questions

1. Why was Joseph so loved by his father and hated by his brothers?

2. What did Joseph do that was the "last straw" for his brothers?

3. How did Potiphar show that he trusted Joseph?

4. How did Joseph end up in prison in Egypt?

5. Describe a time in your life when you were misunderstood and lied about, and how you reacted to it.

6. When Joseph got out of prison, what was his new position?

7. Describe how God has brought blessing into your life through circumstances you did not understand.

8. Although they may not deserve it, whom will you forgive this week?

Memory Verse

And we know that all things work together for good to them that love God, to them who are the called according to his purpose.
—ROMANS 8:28

JONATHAN
True Friendship

Text

1 SAMUEL 18:1–4

1   And it came to pass, when he had made an end of speaking unto Saul, that the soul of Jonathan was knit with the soul of David, and Jonathan loved him as his own soul.

2   And Saul took him that day, and would let him go no more home to his father's house.

3   Then Jonathan and David made a covenant, because he loved him as his own soul.

4   And Jonathan stripped himself of the robe that was upon him, and gave it to David, and his garments, even to his sword, and to his bow, and to his girdle.

Overview

Jonathan was David's best friend in the years before David became king, and he was just the type of friend David needed at the time. In this lesson we'll take a look at how Jonathan strengthened David when he was weak, how he gave to David when he was in need, and how he warned David when he was in danger. These things he did selflessly, and so his example has come down to us as the epitome of what a friend should be.

Lesson Theme

A true friend is a precious gift from God. But as blessed as it is to have a friend, it is a greater blessing to be a friend. As we study the relationship of Jonathan and David, let's take the challenge to be a better friend to our friends.

Introduction

_____

_____

_____

I. _____ Friendship

PROVERBS 17:17

17 A friend loveth at all times, and a brother is born for adversity.

A. _____ DAVID PHYSICALLY

1 SAMUEL 23:16

*16 **And Jonathan Saul's son arose, and went to David into the wood**, and strengthened his hand in God.*

B. _____ DAVID SPIRITUALLY

1 SAMUEL 23:16

*16 And Jonathan Saul's son arose, and went to David into the wood, and **strengthened his hand in God**.*

II. _____ Friendship

A. GAVE HIS _____

1 SAMUEL 18:3–4

3 Then Jonathan and David made a covenant, because he loved him as his own soul.

4 And Jonathan stripped himself of the robe that was upon him, and gave it to David, and his garments, even to his sword, and to his bow, and to his girdle.

B. GAVE HIS _____ ___

1 SAMUEL 23:17

17 And he said unto him, Fear not: for the hand of Saul my father shall not find thee; and thou shalt be king over Israel, and I shall be next unto thee; and that also Saul my father knoweth.

C. GAVE HIS _____

1 SAMUEL 20:4

4 Then said Jonathan unto David, Whatsoever thy soul desireth, I will even do it for thee.

III. _____ Friendship

A. _____

1 SAMUEL 20:19–22

19 And when thou hast stayed three days, then thou shalt go down quickly, and come to the place where thou didst hide thyself when the business was in hand, and shalt remain by the stone Ezel.

20 And I will shoot three arrows on the side thereof, as though I shot at a mark.

21 And, behold, I will send a lad, saying, Go, find out the arrows. If I expressly say unto the lad, Behold, the arrows are on this side of thee, take them; then come thou: for there is peace to thee, and no hurt; as the LORD liveth.

22 But if I say thus unto the young man, Behold, the arrows are beyond thee; go thy way: for the LORD hath sent thee away.

B. _____

Conclusion

Study Questions

1. What was Jonathan's position in the kingdom of Saul?

2. What does the Bible say about Jonathan's friendship for David at the very start of their relationship?

3. Where was David when Jonathan went to strengthen his hand in God?

4. What did Jonathan give to David in order to show his friendship?

5. What was the warning that Jonathan gave David?

6. What can you do strengthen a friend's hand in God this week?

7. What can you do to meet the needs of a friend this week?

8.   If you have a friend who is headed for trouble, will you
     be the one to give a loving warning?

Memory Verse

*And Jonathan Saul's son arose, and went to David into the
wood, and strengthened his hand in God.*—1 SAMUEL 23:16

For additional Christian
growth resources visit
www.strivingtogether.com